The Sunday Naturalist

The Sunday Naturalist

Anthony Sobin

Ohio University Press
Athens, Ohio

LIBRARY
The University of Texas
At San Antonio

© Copyright 1982 by Anthony Sobin
Printed in the United States of America.
All rights reserved.

Library of Congress Cataloging in Publication Data

Sobin, Anthony, 1944-
   The Sunday naturalist.

   I.   Title.
PS3569.O34S9   811'.54   82-6316
ISBN 0-8214-0636-1   AACR2
ISBN 0-8214-0637-X (pbk.)

from, as much as for,

Albert, Arthur and Jon

Contents

PART IV   ARTHUR'S LAST MOVIE

Acknowledgements

Grateful acknowledgement is made to the editors of the following journals and anthologies for first seeing many of these poems into print.

THE AMERICAN POETRY REVIEW (editors: Stephen Berg, David Bonanno, Rhoda Schwartz, Kathleen Sheeder and Arthur Vogelsang): "King René at the Spring," "Sharon, Glum in the Dark Chair, Reads," "The November Suicides," "Propping Up Bodies to Fool the Indians" and "Cabin Fever."

THE BELOIT POETRY JOURNAL (editors: Robert H. Glauber, David M. Stocking and Marion Kingston Stocking): "Fecund Poem," "Concerning Archeology: A Report, A Photograph, A Painting," "The Museum, The Hands," "The Dream of the Moth," "Fear of the Telephone," "Snow Camp," "Thin Air Camp, The La Sal Range," "The Calculation," and "Arthur's Last Movie."

BLUE BUILDINGS (editors: Ruth Doty and Mark Doty): "Zurich: February 5, 1916."

THE FALCON (editors: W. A. Blais and Joe David Bellamy): "Near a Pond, In a Field of Tall Grass, You Think of How You Might Pay."

THE MIDWEST QUARTERLY (editor: Michael Heffernan): "Theodora's Dream."

PANACHE (editor: David R. Lenson): "March Rite: Getting It Up."

THE PARIS REVIEW (editors: Michael Benedikt and George Plimpton) "19th Century Landscape with Pond," "What They Had Come For," "Camouflage in Nature" and "Found Poem: Wind Fells Oklahoma's Ancient Chimney Rock."

PARTISAN REVIEW (poetry editor: John Ashbery): "Study in White," "Photograph: Home for the Aged, Stowe, Vermont— 1911."

POETRY (editors: John Frederick Nims, Daryl Hine): "Wilderness Area," "The Stinkhorn" and "Eating the Bowfin" copyright 1974 and 1979 by The Modern Poetry Association.

POETRY NORTHWEST (editor: David Wagoner): "Picasso Postcard with Pigeons." "Driving Home to See the Folks," and "The Children."

POETRY NOW (editor: E. V. Griffith): "The Winter Sky," "We Decide To Do a Porno Movie."

INTRO 6: LIFE AS WE KNOW IT (editor: George Garrett) Doubleday & Co., New York, 1974.

HEARTLAND II: POETS OF THE MIDWEST (editor: Lucien Stryk) Northern Illinois University Press, 1975.

SELECTIONS—UNIVERSITY POETRY PRIZES 1973-1978 (editor: Stanley Kunitz) The Academy of American Poets, New York, 1980.

Certain of the poems in this volume consist in part of found materials: "Zurich: February 5, 1916" from Martin Esslin's *Theatre of the Absurd* and "Sharon, Glum in the Dark Chair, Reads" from *Rembrandt* by Joseph-Emile Muller.

I would like to thank The National Endowment for the Arts for a fellowship that provided time for the writing of many of these poems.

It is only shallow people who do not judge by appearances. The mystery of the world is the visible, not the invisible.

Oscar Wilde
from a letter

Dream delivers us to dream and there is no end to illusion.
. . . Was it Boscovich who found out bodies never come in contact? Well souls never touch their objects. An innavigable sea washes between us . . . all things swim and glitter. Ghostlike we glide through nature and would not know our place again.

R. W. Emerson
"Experience"

Part I   Concerning Archeology

19TH CENTURY LANDSCAPE WITH POND

You are in an outdoor painting.

In the barnyard
a farmer is forking hay
from an inexhaustible stack
to permanently contented animals.

At the pond
a boy in a flowing blue shirt
is fishing with infinite patience.

But you
are not infinite;

Once
you stood close to the boy, bored,
looking off into the vanishing point
in the yellow and mauve pastures.

But the painter, in a single
moment of dissatisfaction,
pulled the grass up over you

and now, where you are buried,
a cow with an everlasting thirst
drinks from the pond.

PICASSO POSTCARD WITH PIGEONS

I am in light yellow
with the four black stripes
and you are the blue-breasted lovely
with the fan of ochre tailfeathers.

Perched in this high Mediterranean window
at the peak of a cliff
the azure sea spreads beneath us
with its ivory breakers and shivering palms,
olive groves and viridian islands.

I have just said to you
"Oh how like a postcard this is,
or a vacationeer's lighthearted snapshot."
And you are saying to me,
as a lady pigeon would,
"No no, so much more like a painting or
a dream, an early morning dream
dreamt late in life."

And in the midst of this talk
unrecorded by the oils
and out of sight beneath the window ledge

there is a red sailboat made tiny by the ocean.
In it are a striped-shirted man and
a lovely dark woman with pale eyes.
They are thinking nothing of the pigeons

or canvases, left in high studio windows, still wet.
The boat is running full sail against the wind
and the green spray of the ocean
is beading up golden
on the warm yellow skin of their faces.

KING RENÉ AT THE SPRING

after an illumination in *Le Livre
du Coeur de l'Amour Epris*, ca. 1457

In this painting
it is another moonless night.

Desire is asleep in the background
only a dark lump beneath the trees.

At left
the horses are grazing quietly
with the stars so thick and white behind them
that the smallest details of their saddles
are outlined against the sky.

At right, more stars
simmering between the rows
of slender poplars.

It was in the midst of my journey
when I knelt at this spring

and the painter froze me here
head lowered, my lips
about to touch the coal black water
cupped in my hands.

Five hundred years I have been
gazing into this water and each day
I see crouched in my palms

Dame Melancholy, lamentable figure
all in black, trying to warm her clenched hands
over a tiny fire in her hearth
that shimmers on the surface of this black liquid
like a golden coin.

Her voice swirling through the water
whispers to my lips: René,
René we are on the edge
of The Forest of the Long Wait.

Close by
is my page, figure of my strength
and unbroken vitality. Each day
the concern grows in his eyes.

On my left, the red brown horse stands
saddled and ready; his eyes alone
look out of the picture.

Each day I ask the woman in my hands for food.
Each day she holds up to my lips
a piece of grey bread, made
she whispers
from a grain called Hard Want.

FECUND POEM

Old photograph.
A farm
in early spring.

By the fence
female animals
swollen with milk.

In the foreground two aunts
big round stomachs
pregnant and smiling.

The flowers and
their flowers.

Off to one side
Grandmother
holding Mother

wrapped in a towel
like a pitcher of milk.

ZURICH: FEBRUARY 5, 1916

Seventy kilometers away World War I rages on.
It is Zurich, February 5, 1916, and at No. 1
Spiegelgasse, a quiet residential street,
it is opening night at the Cabaret Voltaire.

Tristan Tzara, young Rumanian poet,
screams from his works as Huelsenbeck, drunk,
blindfolds Hugo Ball and opens under his right hand
a French dictionary. Ball's index finger
slides down the page and lights on "dada."

The singer at the cabaret has a new name!
Everyone yells to her, "Dada! Dada! Dada!"
In her honor, Hans Arp, with a sledge hammer,
noisily destroys antique Greek statuary,

followed closely by Kokoschka's play
in which the cure for love is death.
Tzara, backstage, is responsible
for the thunder and lightning as well as
having to say "Anima, Sweet Anima!"
as the voice of the parrot—but he is also
looking after entrances and exits and is
thundering at all the wrong times.

Directly across the street,
in house No. 6 Spiegelgasse,
Lenin tries to read.

SHARON, GLUM IN THE DARK CHAIR, READS

She does not like biographies;
the hero's end is always the same.
And this one is worse;
Rembrandt dies on the first page.
She has skipped to the back—
he's dying again,
"There is no rest for those who do not work
and spend their life in front of easels putting on airs."

The plan is circular with dim light in the middle.
It is still possible to distinguish face, hands and clothes
but the style is more allusive than ever before.
Sitting in the shadows she has a biblical look
though the Bible does not mention her in this scene—
nothing to divert attention from her, no secondary character—
not the least evocation of an architectural framework;
she is practically alone as she holds the book in her hands.

CONCERNING ARCHEOLOGY:
A REPORT, A PHOTOGRAPH, A PAINTING

for Arthur Vogelsang

I. The Archeologists' Report

Mr. Heisig's farm:
Conical mound central on high bluff
over mouth of Turkey River and S.W.
of large animal effigy (prob. an otter).

37 ft. diameter, 3½ ft. high at center.
Brush, trees, some old cultivation.
9-12 inches yellow earth;
ashes in a 2-4 inch layer.

At center, at fourteen inches,
an imperfect dog (?) skull.

Several inches of white clay;
flint chips and a few shards
showing the action of fire.

At original ground level
3 well-preserved Neanderthaloid
skeletons in the sitting posture.
One skeleton (a) facing the east,
the second (b) in front of (a)
and facing it. The third: a few
inches north of (a) facing the north.
Two adults, one younger (or female).

Many relics. A rich grave
(containing possibly all their possessions).

A pipe of carved grey sandstone in the form
of a lynx or panther—eyes of pure native
copper having, at that time, great value.

A small polished stone axe (broken);
near the breast of one
a gorget of blue rocks.

Around (b) five rude scrapers and
about the shoulders and in the skull
of the last are scattered
thirty-one fresh-water pearls.

II. A Photograph of 19th Century Archeologists

Slightly out of focus and deeply yellowed
two males stand on the left and right
made taller by their brushed beaver hats.

It is late afternoon
and in the long exposure
the one on the left has coughed
obliterating most of his face and neck
and all of his right hand.

In the foreground is the grave
with two of the three skeletons visible.

Behind the excavation is the heap
of discarded dirt and behind that
the nameless man on the right stands with
one foot raised, resting it on the debris.

The long shadow of the coat tails
of the man on the left crosses in front
of the group and captures within it
the black shoe of the man on the right,
making visible a thick layer of dust
that has begun to settle on the bright shine.

In the left hand of one man is the stone axe;
in his other hand, held forward cautiously and
fully in focus, are the thirty-one fresh-water
pearls having, at that time, great value.

Between the men, and at the level of their
shoulders, a thin, youngish woman dressed

11

entirely in black glances down and to the right.
Her eyes appear closed as they are caught in the shadow
of her broad hat's great ostrich plume.

A long, narrow and silky-black purse hangs
in front of her, just beneath the waist.
Her long-nailed fingertips hold it there,
curled around its silver chain.

In contrast to the stern men
she carries a thin smile; one that is
in the process of shrinking from its broader
dimensions of a minute ago. She knows that they
have misinterpreted the last words she spoke
and that she must wait this long moment
before explaining.

A brief caption: "In April, 1880, the first excavations
in Northern Iowa were carried out by these three well-
known members of the Society."

Above, and to the left of the figures,
beneath a hovering cloud,
are illegible notations made upon the face
of the photograph in a small dark hand.

III.   *A Painting of 21st Century Archeologists*

Seated around an octagonal table
a more-than-realistic man with ochre hair
is typing on a cadmium-orange typewriter
while, in that small dining room,
seated in front of him and facing him,
a woman whose face is in shadows reads
aloud from a yellowed booklet whose cover:
        "Proceedings of the 34th Meeting
        Western Archeological Society—1881"
can be read in a mirror. On the inner pages
(which the painting allows us to read over
her shoulder) are a report and an early
photograph of three standing figures.

To the left of the ochre typist,
another man (b), his back to us
and the others, is taking a step
through the doorway in the back of the painting
into a kitchen. In his hand he carries
a broad crystal glass empty except for ice cubes
and a bent slice of green lime. Sunlight
passes through the glass projecting a perfect
spectrum on the white refrigerator door.

On the rim of the glass is a pale yellow lip print.
Its tiny crevices are entirely discernible
at a distance at which not even
the lip print should have been visible.
A stout, perfectly preserved baby from
the eruption of Vesuvius sits upright
on the kitchen counter showing the action of fire.
On one of the man's fingers curled around
the glass there is a tiny drop of blood
where the man has been biting his fingernails.
A baker is prostrate on the kitchen floor in exactly
the position he fell while baking bread.

From the mirror behind the man with the ochre
hair we learn that he is typing a report
on the group's recent expedition to Egypt.
As we read we learn that:

      the tour guide has just taken them aside
      and for a price, which he holds crumpled
      in his small dark hand, tells
      the archeologists that the pyramid, deep
      within which they are now standing,
      is unique in that every hour for five
      thousand years one of the hieroglyphs
      (high above them on the tomb wall)
      mysteriously transforms itself into a
      small dark bird-like woman who emerges
      slowly from the stone but once free
      drops to the floor and runs off at
      tremendous speed like a black heron,
      down a long sandstone passageway.
      "As one looks up at it," he has just

written, "the wall where half of the
hieroglyphs are missing appears as an
unfinished page of typing . . ."

In the pause, the sharp-featured woman who was
reading aloud is looking hard at the man who
is typing. She is about to begin speaking a
new word. His index finger, on its way down,
hovers like a cloud over one key.

After a time a slight breeze passes over
the table—upsetting her stare and the
incredible feats of patience she has been
performing with her lips and eyes. He
pretends not to have understood her last words.

Illuminated by the rainbow between the glass
and the refrigerator, a cloud of stringy particles
can be seen hovering in the air and beginning
to settle on the black tile floor like ashes.
The man with the ochre hair is about to say
dig all you like.

THE MUSEUM, THE HANDS

for Albert Goldbarth

I.

The darkened *Sixteenth Century English Room* floated
stone by stone across the Atlantic then fell back
into just the right shape dead-center U.S.A.
The entire length of the long-board and eight oak chairs
are cold and still waiting in front of the carved stone fireplace
(with plywood false back and sides) for the scullery maids
to come with a coal from a peasant fire to rekindle the flames
that were allowed to die during this exceptionally long night.

I focus on the dents and furrows of the table, evidence
for what must have been centuries of brawls and platters
sliding under heavy English meals of forest game. Everywhere
    signs
are telling us that we cannot run our late 20th Century hands
even lightly through the old scars or across the medieval
    tapestry's
images of fragile people in a garden looking happy and afraid—
their long gothic fingers made from single brown threads.

I hold out in front of me this image, this
evidence for a hand and I watch as my thumb skims
across what must be my fingertips, one by one. Any touch
and my own marks, my heraldry, would give me away;
my name would slip down the swirling lines into a summoner's
    ear
and I, like everyone, would be betrayed by my own hand.

II.

In *Archaeology*, a half-yard deep in the wall and behind thick
    glass,

15

is the gift from Sweden: the deep brown human hand of the Iron
        Age
Woman of Windeby Fen, found perfect in a Scandinavian bog,
        A.D. 1947,
clad only in the last traces of what must have been a short linen
        tunic
reddish hair curling to well beneath the waist—

"This statuesque young woman of 18 or 19 years, clearly an
extraordinary beauty in her own time, was divided carefully after
this photograph was taken and shipped across the Atlantic
to several North American museums. It is thought that the iron
of her belt, bracelets and jewelry dissolved in the bog water
and preserved her intact—giving away her exact appearance
at the time of her death, quite early in the Iron Age."

Today her fingertips would leave clearer prints than
my own, pressed against the glass—solid evidence
for an entire body, a life, clearer to me than my own.
The half-inch thickness of cold glass protects the hands
from one another like the span of two thousand-years—like the
        width
of the Atlantic Ocean before there were ships to cross it.

III.

On display in *Paleontology* is the huge slab of petrified sea floor
separated carefully and carried away intact from a fossil ocean—
"Each half-inch of strata represents roughly two thousand
        years."
Clear impressions offer solid evidence for the lives of the extinct,
the curling patterns in the mud of burrowing sea worms,
the death masks of trilobites like fingerprints of the Paleozoic.
In the dents and furrows we can focus on the outlines of their
        bodies
just as they were at death, before there was an Atlantic Ocean.

Last year's student, a woman who will always be too young
        for me,
stands intensely watching the display as if something
were happening in it—as if it were the movie at the drive-in
complete with plot and action. As she looks up and sees me

16

my old recurring dream flashes by—the one that always ends
with Queen Bess ordering me beheaded and quartered, the
        dream
which always begins cloudy, with me watching intensely,
as if through a half-inch layer of translucent bog water,
tiny worms curling under my fingernails like thin brown
        threads,
their trails beginning to fall into just the right patterns—
my own hands beginning to give me away. She is happy to
        see me,

and tells me all about her European summer, her new car and
        lover
and art history paper she's in the middle of—the one concerning
Michaelangelo's "Creation" far out on the Sistine Chapel
        ceiling.
We talk about how "unpainterly and statue-like the figures are,
yet how they nonetheless seem real in spite of their look of being
frozen there in stone." Only I am uneasy. It's cold she says
and jokes about wishing they'd start a huge fire in the *English
        Room*.
I focus on her hair and her hand curling the bracelet at her
        wrist.
I measure with my eye the hard transparent distance between us
        and
hear her asking me if I know the statistics—the ratio in a
        lifetime
of the things we can see to the things we can touch.

Part II   Fear of the Telephone

DEPARTURE AT DUSK:
AIRPORT CORRIDORS, THE LATE AUTUMN PLANE

Goodbye friends in your hiding places
wearing your coats of fleece and looking to the sky.
Autumn has disappeared to the south
and I can see you from this airplane window settled
for the winter into hawthorn thickets growing smaller
holding hands with your sexy girlfriend the night.

Over the ridge, over your eyes caged in branches,
endless flights of birds black out the sky, their shadows
flickering across the stream just north of you
where three dead sheep are fading into the soil—
fading away to bones and thick white coats
and sinking into the layers of earth beneath them
where the slow hearts of moles beat in controlled death
down the long corridors of sleep.

Ha! Already I can hear you in my memory
your footsteps walking away down airport corridors
like the echoes of a lost watch.
The sounds fade and disappear
like a vapor trail across the night sky.
Don't you know yet how things are?
You migrate, you hibernate or you die!
How can you expect me to love you when you
can't understand nature's simplest laws?

No! Don't you dare wave to me! Goodbye
you ridiculous fast-breathing padded bones
I can no longer bear saying goodbye to.

THE DREAM OF THE MOTH

Only when your eyes
grow accustomed to the dark
do you begin to notice
the two yellow lights
hovering at arm's length
over the hills of your bed.

And then you realize
they are your own fingertips
glowing where they lifted the moth
by its wings
that afternoon
in the field by the house.

Trying to rub one another clean
the fingertips themselves
seem in flight over the dark blankets
though the light has gone deep into the skin
and will not brush away.

Later, in your dream,
the two spots of light have become
the two lit windows of a house
standing in a black field—
a house which draws you
irresistibly toward it.

And when your legs
will not carry you there fast enough
your thumb and finger
break from your hand
and flutter away
leaving you behind, collapsed
and gasping in the wet grass.

You can see them in the distance now
a dark shape butting against

22

the glass of the windows
but inside the house someone
turns out the light and
closes the door behind him and soon

you feel two enormous fingerprints
of pressure moving across your back,
pinching your shoulder-blades together,
and it's then you know
this is your last dream, the one
you will never fly away from.

THE NOVEMBER SUICIDES

M.S., Salt Lake City, Nov. 3
D. McC., Wichita, Nov. 4

Suicides, like those growing too old,
know the feeling of the earth
turning beneath them

and we see them everywhere
holding on to bus stops or the backs
of chairs to keep from falling.

But this month nothing
seems strong enough.
You are falling

like the white sheets of desk calendars
pulled across your faces
like the eyelid of night, a dark shutter
locking you forever into a last picture
that will blur with time.

You are falling
like the leaves of November
coming to rest a thousand miles apart
but in the same layer of earth

and in the grave beneath your graves
the entire Iron Age stretches around the earth
rusted away to a single black layer
no thicker than an eyelid or a shadow.

****

It is so much as if we simply left you
at a party forgetting to say goodbye
then somehow just never saw you again.

24

We put books in the library
for you and write a poem and in time
we will return to these cities and
across a room glimpse a face
we think is yours and even start toward you
forgetting for our first few steps
that you were ever dead.

But it is only a small shadow
passing across our memory
as the night our second moon
revolves around the earth
marking off our time
and blurring our faces.

And in the years to come when for no reason
we crawl from the layers of our beds
and go to the curtain

it is you we'll be looking for in the night.
The shadows you no longer cast
have gone into its making

and your faces dissolving there
hold for us
such a fine strangeness now

that our shadows
are beginning to think of us
as their shadows.

NEAR A POND, IN A FIELD OF TALL GRASS, YOU THINK OF HOW YOU MIGHT PAY

Stand around all day in a field of tall grass
in the hot skin of being very tired
and watch a huge rectangular night begin
closing in on you from the east as if you
were a thin letter all signed and folded.

A pale darkness first. The mist rises off a small pond
which, like you, is never to be seen again.
It will erase the trees of the far bank
and you will no longer be able to tell
which song is the cricket, which is the frog,
whether it's cattle just over the ridge
grazing, or horses, while the nighthawks
scoop up what light is left and
swallow it down in long sweeping dives.

It is all set in motion now. What has been
sailing captive for years through the veins,
the boat made from the hollow bones of birds,
will soon come bursting out, will sail home
on the flood of all that has been contracted,
all that is to be paid on time, everything you owe.

And it is growing closer—
the boat's beams are numb bones now, and you
are dazed and growing sleepy and are beginning
to lose touch now, even with the bank, the creditors
(all those years of interest they claim they will lose)
the lovers, the ex-friends, standing about you in the dark—
the many who will hold it against you
for paying, all at once,
what they kept saying they wanted all along.

PROPPING UP BODIES TO FOOL THE INDIANS

It is your birthday.
Another man falls dead at your feet

and his body is like a shadow
that stretches out from your black shoes.

You pick him up from behind
grasping him beneath the shoulders
and clasp your hands across his chest
until your hands begin to look
like his hands folded in death.

Then you drag him toward a covered wagon
your face buried in his wet red hair
breathing the smell of his worry
and already he seems
almost too heavy for you
as if you were lifting
more than your own weight.

His heels dragging in the sand
leave ruts like the wagon tracks
that start in Virginia and now
cross the plains of Kansas, half way there.

You jerk the arrow out from between his ribs
but the head stays behind
to float for years through the cavity of his chest
a shrunken and petrified heart.

But no matter.
You prop him against a wagon wheel
alongside the others, facing the enemy.
Soon the Indians will learn how hopeless this is;
for each one of us they kill
another will come to fill his place.

You weave his arm between two spokes,
jam a carbine into his shoulder
and let his head flop down on the barrel
taking aim forever
from his place in the circle of wagons.

Far down the line is the handful of infants,
useless, drooling, self-indulgent,
and then there is the gang of boys with slingshots
the leather pulled back, touching each of their cheeks
just beneath the right eye.

Then come the men in their twenties
as if in a room of a wax museum.
You have posed this group after Giotto's *Lamentation*
though each figure is holding a six-gun
and one is also drinking from a bottle of rye.

Your masterpiece, though, is the man at thirty
set apart, nonchalant, without even a gun—just
showing the Indians how fearless we all are.
You have him leaning against the chuck wagon,
hands cupped to his face, frozen there by death
as if calmly lighting a cigar.

CABIN FEVER

Outside
the shadow of a dog
bays at the moon
then sinks deep into the snow,
that smartass hibernating water.

So in the spring
what will come of this?
Will a tiny spotted lake of water
appear on the ground
vaguely dogshaped?
Will a throaty whimper
thaw and float up toward a star?

Well here are the hard cold facts.
Beneath the snow
even now the heavier dog bones
are soaking ever so surely
through the bottom layers of fur
and when spring comes
there will be a circle of grass
somewhat greener than the rest

and that's all.

And now it's so cold outside
the sparrows are decomposing in flight
or committing suicide
against the walls of the house.

Inside
an angry black shadow
is fluttering on my windowsill
beneath where I have hung her cage.

She is flapping her black cape

and screeching like a rusty victrola.
She is puffing like a Victorian sofa.

And I am thinking hard about opening
that little wire door.

DRIVING HOME TO SEE THE FOLKS

Asleep at the wheel nearly
dead I think
and feeling nothing
but the dark eyes of the Wyoming antelope
on my skin—watching me pass—a small animal
growling down the highway
with both eyes aglow.

To keep awake
I push my head out the window
as into a guillotine
the black wind and sleet
slipping under each eyelid
like a child's thin silver spoon.

Looking back into the car
through the ice and tears
I do not recognize that body sleeping there.
I no longer know that leg pressed hard
to the gas, that blue coat or wool scarf or
that hand reaching out to the wheel.

Folks, you know I am doing my best—
pushing hard toward you
through this winter sky
but reduced to this—

just this head out a window
streaming through space like a bearded rock,
a hunk of pocked iron with melting eyes.

The trail of fiery mist
growing out from the back of my head
stretches now for miles across the night.

The odds, I know, are a thousand to one
I'll burn up before touching earth

but if somehow I do make it home
smashing across the farmyard
and lighting up the sky

I will throw a red glow across the barn's silver roof
and crash into the rough wood of your back door
smaller than a grain of sand
making its one childlike knock.

The porch light will hesitate
then snap on, as it always does
when a car comes up the lane
late at night.

The two sleepy old faces
will come to the door
in their long soft robes—
will stand there bewildered
rubbing their eyes
looking around and wondering
who it was at their door

no sooner come than gone

a cinder in the eye.

THE WIDOW'S HOUSE

Sits heavier
on its foundation
now

but nobody sees this.

The lamps in the windows
burn just as bright.

The furnace pumps warm air
just as before

just as in that November
they first stepped inside
he kicking snow off his boots
she, curled in a cloud of arms,
a crescent moon drifting across a new sky.

The floors were full of spring then
beneath their steps

but now, in the core of each board
a shaft of lead grows and spreads

and one by one
the shingles break from the roof
and fly into the night.

Crows come to roost in their place
and in time there is a roof of crows
like a heavy black snow that breathes.

The rafters cry beneath their unbearable weight.
The attic windows burst;
the cellar door groans and splits.

And inside
beneath the trembling ceilings
life moves slowly.
A step into the bathroom now
is a cold cemetery walk—
each tiny white tile
has grown a name and a date,
a standing angel or winged skull.

And when night comes
all the wings begin their slow beating—
the crows' wings, the angels' wings
the wings of the moonfaced skulls

all beating downward toward the earth
pushing the house before them

the mud curling beneath the bottom bricks
the nails choking in their boards
the house sinking and sinking
beneath the awful tonnage of absence.

MARCH RITE: GETTING IT UP

Spring in Iowa comes in three days
unfreezing the horse turds
steaming loose all the smells
of fields and hay and drying barn wood
obscuring the skeletons in the trees
of last autumn's ill-fated kites
or last century's ill-fated Negroes
softening up the road kills
for the slow-moving yellow carcass trucks.

And the rasping sound of the workman's
shovel scraping the fur from the concrete
repeats itself.
And the obscene expressions on
the deflated opossums are always the same.
AND the kinds of dead dogs
even begin to repeat themselves, (in three-year cycles OR

maybe it's just every three miles
along the highway).
AND the cupped yellow bulb flowers poke up
through the snow to surprise us *so much* by their
mere presence in all that winter
but, on second thought,
they *do* look sort of dangerous and,
as always, we remark:
"too much like warheads."

So we rush inside to the safety of drinks
and movies—worn out silent films, our lives
repeating themselves—Chaplin and Keaton breathless
chasing, being chased, running north speeding south,
film breaking on the hot teeth of projector gears,
shredding, curling high into the air, but being driven on
by the projector, floating, at times almost motionless . . .
Wait! This is all film I have watched before!
I shut my eyes. I try to remember the outcome . . .
I could grow hard trying to remember.

35

FEAR OF THE TELEPHONE

When, after all those years of being afraid,
you suddenly realize that those telephones
endlessly ringing
are only the sound effects
in this, the soft, funny movie of your life,
you can finally relax and begin to enjoy it.

Now,
when the telephone goes off like a cliché,
each ring a clean white row of teeth,
you rush to it smiling
even if you're dripping with bath water
or out of breath from love.

It may be one of those calls
you always hang up on, like
the job offer from New York too good to be true
or, at four in the morning,
the frightened, childlike voice at your ear
of a woman you don't know
who confesses her love for you
and then pulls the trigger.

Ha! What a good story, you say,
though your ear is still ringing.
You are really beginning
to appreciate this.

You become polite to wrong numbers
even if they've called before
and when your friends come
whispering their worst fears to you
through the black wire
you agree with them—yes, you conclude,
suicide *would* seem your best bet.

And when your brother calls,
in desperate trouble
bleeding in a highway phone booth,
you tell him to stay put,
that you won't waste a minute, then
slowly you take off your clothes
settle into a steaming hot bath
and later drift off to sleep
in the television's soft soothing light.

Later, hours past midnight,
when the bells start ringing death
and draw you from your bed in the dark

you seem shaken by the news;
you make your voice tremble
then, slowly
you lay the black bone back in its cradle
and have a good hard laugh! You say:

Ah, telephone,
old ventriloquist
you've learned so many
of the voices I love.

How far away you make them seem!

You could almost make me believe
this wire in my hand truly stretches
those thousands of miles
to within an inch of their lips.

Such good stories you tell.
By now, I could almost love you,
your cold black muzzle
pressed against my ear
about to whisper.

Part III   The Sunday Naturalist

THE WINTER SKY

We come home at three
after drinking all night
at The Great Bear Bar

and with the lights just out,
our watery heads buried in pillows,
the cat tromps across your sleepy frame
wanting to be petted, her cold feet
pressing hollows into your breasts.

You scratch her ears
the sides of her face
and thousands of quiet sparks
begin flowing through her fur.

Suddenly she is a black meadow in summer
alive with fireflies.

Her pale light
streams across your body
lighting its plains and ridges
its crevices and
its swells;

you can see it now, can't you?
low on the horizon—
the shimmering outline
of the head, the pointed ears
the long curving tail,

Constellation "The Cat"
bright in the winter sky.

WHAT THEY HAD COME FOR

Getting ten thousand feet "closer to nature"
by Desolation Trail
they had *seen* their breath in mid-July.

Then, heading back down,
she kneels in deep moss
to drink from a stream,
her curled hands numb as a tin cup
against her cheeks as icy water
drips down the overheated skin
between her breasts.

He sinks both his thumbs hard
into the hot cheeks of an orange
and pulls the large-pored skin away
piece by piece,

and from his dripping fingertips the strings
of white netting fall into the breeze
and float away like drifting nerves.

How carefully
she separates the sections
as if dissecting
a protozoan colony or miniature sun
lifted from the surface of the stream

and taking the seeds from her lips
one by one
like the nuclei of broken cells
she lines them up on a huge flat boulder
Pluto, Neptune, Uranus, Saturn . . .
for the sun to dry.

WILDERNESS AREA

Climbing the high trails
panting the thin air
we are surrounded
by countless invisible hunts.
Few victims ever escape
and those that do
always bear the tiny scars
of hooked feet and tight mandibles.

They will never be safe
from tomorrow's enemies
or even the dangers
of their own short lifespans
which grow quietly like stones
in the pits of their fleeing bodies.

Our legs grow heavy with the thought of it.
There is no place here safe enough to rest—
where we might avoid looking down
looking down and seeing ourselves
breathless and shrinking, bleeding uncontrollably
through all the closed tubes of our bodies.

SNOW CAMP

Rivers of stars

February's skeleton
glowing white above us
with its bones of solid ice.

Stars
pockets of heat
turning in frigid space.

Out there
too cold for life
or far too hot.

And here
flames rise and fall against our faces
against the small white tent
and the walls of snow surrounding us.

We sit by the campfire
planets around a huge sun
bodies half in day
and half in night.

Here
there is no middle ground.
The air freezes
right up to the flames themselves
and you have pulled your knees
tight to your chest
bundled against the cold.

I think of what it would be
to speak one word too few
or too many,
to reach over and touch
for one moment too long
the bones of your cheek.

In front of us the stones glow red.
The stones behind us would freeze to the skin
and in such narrow spaces
we learn to have our lives
we learn
to touch everything lightly
and I know
if I press too hard
against your fiery skin
I will feel the cold rise up
from the ice-crusted bones below.

THIN AIR CAMP, THE LA SAL RANGE

Mountains blending with the clouds,

steam from the coffee
blending with the mist.

The second orange tent
fifty meters through the fog
is passing in and out of sight

and you are still asleep,
one bare shoulder out of the sleeping bag
strands of your pale hair
lacing through the ground frost.

I am staring off downstream, nearly awake,
where the cluster of lodgepole pines
drifts back and forth out of the fog

and at first there are just the trees
but then there are the trees and
a single doe beneath them
floating in grey air
grazing noiselessly
not looking up.

Her coat is nearly white
for the winter;
its borders blending into the air,
the air into the trees;

in time
her black eyes might seem
only pine cones against the snow

and I think
she couldn't possibly be alive:

46

legs so thin they disappear
before reaching the ground,
the motionless ears, the still eyes,
the enormous red wound in her white shoulder.

But in the time it takes to wake you
she's gone

back into the other world

leaving us here alone
with our hands around our coffee

so half awake

passing in and out of our lives.

THE STINKHORN

When she was young the shrewd stinkhorn
covered her body with a fetid brown paste
rank with the stench of rotting flesh.

Then all avoided her save the fawning flies.
They swarmed to her side, doffing their caps
bowing and smiling, then leaned closer
and whispered sweetly in her ear.

She lowered her head, feigned a blush
then let them take what they would.

But once they had picked her clean
the flies laughed at her uncomeliness
then droned away joking in a thousand directions,
to barns and pastures and far-away mountains.

*   *   *

In less than a day the paste had killed each one
and the stinkhorn's spores took root
wherever a false friend fell.

Today, though she bares only
the faint sweet fragrance of butter,
nothing alive dares to touch her

and she grows rich in her days
knowing that no one will ever guess
how succulent, how sweet,
her fine white flesh has always been.

THEODORA'S DREAM

Outside your window
are the pine forest
and the stream flowing by;
all night
it has been raining
a cold night rain
and one by one
the mushrooms have been pushing up
through the loam.

As I look in on you still asleep
beneath the layers of dark covers
the picture I see in that half-light
stops me cold—

a scene from my worst
dreams of dismemberment:
your head on a pillow, severed—
your body simply gone.

In this world
only your face remains—

your face and hair
and beneath your eyelids
the ripples of dreams
flowing past.

But somehow you remain calm
as if confident of a good end
and then you are standing beside me
taking my hand

and we watch you there asleep
dreaming without fear

and take ease;
we remember that it's *all* just a dream

that nothing we see
stays real for very long.

And as the room fills with light
and as you open your eyes and
pull back the covers
you are there complete

as if your body had grown back overnight
on the forest floor
after a rain.

EATING THE BOWFIN

Old atavist, ugly paleozoic fish

tired of climbing the evolutionary ladder
and waiting for something good to come along
like feet or a pair of lungs

one year you just stepped off
and let the others rush on by—

so much like the gold miner
galloping through Utah in '49
who pitched his tent for one night
and stayed sixty years.

He axed his wagons into slats and hubs
made them into windmills
and dug down into the business of living.

And do you ever wonder—what if
you *had* climbed all the way to the top
like the sleek maniac salmon, the men,
the whole jittery collection of thoroughbreds?

Would you be found today
only in tiny glacial pools at treeline,
grown small, perfect and jewel-like,
a brilliant spectrum fluttering between sunken rocks?

Pressing your sweet yellow flesh
to the roof of my mouth,
feeling you dissolve there
like a transfusion
at the top of my spine,
I know you did the right thing.

For the next twenty-four hours
your cells will power

the finest movements of my hands,
each breath and step I take

as if you had claimed my feet, my lungs
for your own; as if
it was you who had eaten me.

For these few hours the thoughts
that pass through my skull
come more like dreams—flashes of silver
up from deep water or a ponderous
reddish swirl when the really old blood
rises to the surface
and takes a gulp of air.

Each muscle of my body is sinking to the bottom
and burrowing in, smooth and silver,
basking there in your life
the sweet power of surrender
the strength of staying the same.

Part IV   Arthur's Last Movie

WE DECIDE TO DO A PORNO MOVIE

As we yawn and play two-handed rummy
in front of the picture window, you notice
how brightly we're reflected in the glass
against the black background of night.

So I take the part of *The Boss Behind the Desk*
while you become *The Busty Secretary*. How closely
we watch ourselves as you giggle, straddle
my lap and bounce obscenely up and down.

Then you turn your head so we're both facing
the audience; we roll our eyes in huge lascivious
circles and let our tongues hang and wiggle.
With exaggerated slyness I pull up your sweater

and give them a little peek while you
titillate them with manipulations performed
just out of sight beneath the desk.
Earlier, an occasional moth would flutter by,

glance in at us, then move along.
But now there are hundreds at the glass, clamoring,
rushing the screen, clawing to get in, forgetting
that it's all just a movie in here.

VALENTINE APART

February 14
somewhere, years ago
it is 3 a.m.
in the heartless light
of the all-night diner
where people come to sober up.
You are fourteen or fifteen at best
looking strangely dark-skinned and foreign
in a turquoise booth, head on the shoulder
of a rough boy in a motorcycle jacket
who smells of semen and cheap leather.

You are not yet as beautiful
as you will become
and I know my hands
will stay strangers to your skin for years
but I am butting into this scene anyway.

I am the anonymous man in the khaki uniform
kneeling in the entryway shadows
mechanically loading the cigarette machine.

And in time, as if in a slow motion film,
you are up and following the sleepy boy out
through the fluorescent glare and country music
your eyes soft stones
a hand's width above the whisper
of lipstick he's left on your mouth
far too red for your age or pure white dress.

A golden heart, engraved "Roughrider,"
flashes from your throat

and as you brush behind my back
in the narrow entryway
I am the man who spins suddenly around
and blocks your path—

who looks you straight in the eyes
even as the carton of Marlboros is still
disappearing beneath your coat.

I am the man who leans into your body
and whispers
      I'll forget what I just saw
      if you promise you'll meet me later
the red cigarettes pounding hard
against the small sharp points of your breasts
half an inch from your heart.

CAMOUFLAGE IN NATURE

*Hidden in this photograph of thick
jungle are four enemy snipers—
How many can you find?*

U.S.M.C. Training Bulletin

To get the drop on the clerk
at the Munger Branch Post Office
we stand in profile perfectly still
against the bulletin board
taking up positions among the prowlers,
the Black Panthers, the urban guerrillas.

We wear the dull expressions
of those being photographed
against their will
and match the lights and greys
of our likenesses
to those of the posters
until flies, sensing no life in us,
light on our faces.

The clerk lifts his head
and stares right at us.
We stop breathing. He looks hard;
shakes his head as if to clear it,
blinks several times, then
quietly goes back to counting
endless sheets of postage.

It's worked! It's worked!
We slide off the wall
and into the street—embracing,
drunk with success. We can be seen
dancing away down the long sidewalk
growing smaller and smaller
among the thick red leaves of October

and as the moments wear on, we grow tiny
our shadows intensify, our borders bleed,
our bodies turn the colors of autumn
until we disappear entirely
between the huge bright dots of the world.

THE CHILDREN

One morning
the old sailor woke
with his hand clutching his throat
like a starfish
wet and cold.

Gasping
he pried the thing loose
finger by finger
then chopped it off

chopped the cold hand into pieces
and threw it overboard.

But on the ocean floor
each finger grew a new hand
each hand grew a new man
and soon they were big enough
to build a boat
just like the old sailor's boat.

They filled the hull
with the air of their lungs
and when it surfaced
they sailed it smartly to the harbor.

Everyone they met they asked
"Have you seen the old sailor?"
"The old sailor, does he live near here?"

When finally they found him
in the dim light of the Seafarer's Inn
he was lifting a cold glass to his lips
with his one remaining hand.

They rushed toward him.
They folded their five bodies around him.

"Father," they all said as one—
their cold breath
spilling from their mouths
and down his cheek—

"Father!" they cried
kissing him and kissing him.

STUDY IN WHITE

The photographer is going all out
for a study in white.

He hopes for a silky, crowlike negative
with layers upon layers of black
spreading from edge to edge.

So for his setting
he has chosen an old farm kitchen
in a far northern province
on a perfect winter day.

For background there are only
the plain whitewashed walls
and the cold snowlight
pouring into the room
through the high windows.

The picture's single figure,
central in the frame,
is a French nun in white habit

who, at the photographer's direction,
has removed with a straight razor
her long black eyebrows

and stands now at a scrubbed pine table
behind the four ivory-colored eggs
he has placed there in the white light
that flows through the clear pitcher of milk
positioned just to her left.

From out of a linen sack
she has just withdrawn two great handfuls of flour
and these she holds out before her
filling the whole center of the frame.

At the moment the shutter snaps open
she is exploring the powder
with her lowered eyes
as if searching for the secret of bread.

The photographer is jubilant!

The negative in its wash
looks like a thin slice of coal

but as he holds it up to the window
the darkness between the nun's black hands
begins to burn with a thousand points of light
as if she were holding all the stars
of a winter night.

"Weevils," he cries. "The flour! Full of weevils!"

And that's not the worst.

There is a moon in that sky too
burning round and fierce above the stars.

The model posing as the nun
has left one of her dark brown eyes open
and light pours through it now
like a stream of milk

as if the shutter had caught her
just in the midst of a wink.

PHOTOGRAPH: HOME FOR THE AGED
STOWE, VERMONT—1911

The men whisper flirtatiously with the women
believing no one can hear them
among the oaks and stone benches
of the back gardens

and in this picture
the eyes of the old men are such a clear blue
that you believe you could walk up the path
right into them—

the blue spreading out around you
like an azure sky in summer
buzzing with wasps and sunlight
and the too sweet smell of ripe pears.

And suddenly you remember everything
as if a door swung open
to some lost childhood home—

the soft floors of honey pine
the fruit jars full of sea-green light
the perfume at the windows
from the gardens and orchards.

You remember how the caretakers would
cut the chrysanthemums back all summer
to make them bloom in fall
and go right on blooming into winter
until their blossoms sank slowly beneath the snow
like drowning men.

Even now the first icy grains can be heard
falling like sand into dry leaves.
The crystals catch in the bronze and russet petals
and do not melt.

The women look up to the sky
through their white hair
and the men take them in their arms
and begin to waltz them slowly homeward
as if to music only they can hear.

The women's gowns billow and enter
the indigo trees like rustling shadows
hems brushing over the fallen pears
grotesque brown lumps in the snow.

All this
in one long New England evening
in a twilight that lasts and lasts
beyond all reason.

All you can hear are their silver bodies
curving through the dark air homeward

and the soft urgent buzzing
from deep inside the rotting pears—
wasps burrowed in and still alive.

It is all like a whisper inside the brain
not unpleasant
but which will not go away.

THE CALCULATION

*Given a constant velocity and the
exact location of two points on a
continuum, the time required to
traverse the distance between them
may easily be calculated as may the
absolute time at one point provided
the same for the other is known.*

—Kurt Hauptmann
Astronomy 1797

It is touching that I don't know for sure
whether today is Saturday or Friday.
I'm sitting at my desk *early* in the morning
biting my nails and blowing the chips
against the landlord's wall.
I am crying softly because it is, for sure,
not Sunday and there is, for sure, no NFL game
until at least tomorrow—and even then this
miserable Salt Lake City T.V. doesn't broadcast the Redskins
(Will my aging father back in Washington, who watched
with me through twenty lean years of Sundays, screaming
at the picture tube "Put in Bukich—why won't they ever
put in Bukich!" when even as a child I knew that Eddie
LeBaron was doing as well as any quarterback could, given
that lousy team, live to see the Washington Redskins win a
Super Bowl?)
but rather lets the signals from the East just zoom by overhead
to disappear forever in space. In the sky this Sunday, only a
dozen feet over my roof, the plays of the three-hour game
will stream by like weather, the line-backers red-dogging
through breaks in the clouds like horses in an apocalyptic
painting
and I'll be sitting down here not knowing a thing about it
until the highlights are shown on the news, hours later.

I think hard about yesterday for any clue to its identity
so that by a rational Eighteenth Century process I could make
a definitive deduction about this one late Twentieth Century
    day.
I cry harder and wish for snow to fall from the charged clouds
to freeze all that motion out the window and deaden things
like a shot. The powerful stadium-shaped dishes on the planets
of distant galaxies are at this moment still picking up
the Redskins of the fifties and sixties. A lot they know.
If it should happen that today is Saturday, then right now
Eddie LeBaron is fishing on the Chesapeake Bay, retired and
growing old, his hand poised behind his head about to make
a *long* cast.

At this moment one of the super sensitive antennae Out There
is receiving the Redskins-Browns game of Sunday, Jan. 15, 1959.
The speed of light being a universal constant, if I knew just
    where
that signal was right now, today would be a simple calculation,
    but
I don't, and it isn't, and we are in the last quarter, and all their
Redskin fans are plenty worried and drinking their kind of beer
    fast.
At this very second, Eddie's arm is cocked somewhere about to
    throw
the game-losing interception, and is frozen in that pose forever,
hurtling past planet, planet and planet, like a painting,
a painting of the only believable life after death.

FOUND POEM:
WIND FELLS OKLAHOMA'S ANCIENT CHIMNEY ROCK

WANOKA (AP) Chimney Rock, which stood for centuries on the Oklahoma plain as a towering guide for covered wagons crossing the treacherous Cimarron River, has fallen victim to the same forces which created it. "Moisture and wind, the tools that sculpted it, reduced the eerie formation to a heap of rubble," said Ernie Crumpler, Oklahoma University geologist.

"I've fished these parts all my life," said Abe Finley, long-time Wanoka fisherman, "and anymore, with old Chimney Rock gone, I can't get my bearings."

Mr & Mrs Marvin Decker, a ranch couple on their way to feed their cattle, were the first to see that the geological oddity no longer stood in its accustomed place. "He said, 'Chimney Rock's gone,'" Mrs Decker said Thursday. "I was looking the other direction and thought oh it's only hidden by dust in the air, but I looked over and sure enough the only thing you could see was a bump on the hill."

"It's quite an experience to look at something you've seen all your life and suddenly you can't even tell where it was," Mrs Decker said, turning to go feed their cattle. She was the first to see that her husband, Marvin Decker, no longer stood in his accustomed place. "He said 'I'm over here,'" Mrs Decker said Thursday. "I was looking the other direction," she explained, "and all I could see was a heap of rubble." "It's because they couldn't get their bearings with old Chimney Rock gone," O.U. geologist Crumpler said, hidden by dust in the air.

It was believed that the chimney, which stood fifty or sixty feet tall, fell during a wind storm about noon on Tuesday. Crumpler said, "As no one witnessed its birth there was no one to see it go. Heavy winter snows and recent torrential rains apparently weakened the base and the wind blew it down."

"It has always been one of our prominent landmarks," said Mrs Louise Fisher, editor of the *Weeds County Enterprise* here. "It's like a big chunk of our early history is now gone."

As Mrs Decker turned around to go feed their cattle, she was the first to see that her husband, Marvin Decker, no longer stood in his accustomed place. "Crumpler said, 'Marvin's gone,'" Mrs

Decker said Thursday. "I was looking the other direction and thought oh I've just lost my bearings or he's hidden by dust in the air, but I looked over and the only thing you could see was Marvin collapsed there like a heap of rubble."

Abner Moss, Weeds County coroner, said that heavy winter snows and recent torrential rains, coupled with the shock of losing Chimney Rock, probably weakened his condition so much that a gust of wind and moisture blew him over about noon on Thursday. "But," he said, "because of dust in the air, no one there could see him go."

"The fallen victim has always been one of our prominent citizens," Editor Fisher said. Mrs. Edna Decker, Decker's mother, reminisced about her son on her way to feed their cattle. "Why, I remember once when he was just a baby, a rock from our tumbledown chimney fell on him. I was looking the other direction," she said, "but sure enough, when we pulled off his little cap, the only thing you could see was a bump on his head." "Today, you can't even see where it was," Decker's wife added. "It's quite an experience to look at something you've seen all your life and suddenly you can't even see where it was."

"It's a real oddity," Crumpler called in an eerie voice from the direction of the treacherous Cimarron River, hidden by dust in the air. "Anymore, around here, nothing's going to be the same," Mrs. Fisher added. Mrs. Decker said "Thursday, if you want to get your bearings."

ARTHUR'S LAST MOVIE

Man in torn coat walks down theatre aisle,
puts out cigarette,
sits down.

Rest of audience settles down;
house lights dim;
film starts;
theme comes up.

On the screen
big screen audience
take their seats, settle down;
house lights dim;
their movie starts:

Camera pans huge expanse of snow, white sky and dwarf pines.

Silence.

Hero appears in distance, out of focus, a round black dot.

Hero in torn coat stumbles through snow toward camera
—inches closer and closer until
entire screen is filled with bottom half of hero's big face.

Screen audience mutters aesthetic disapproval.

Wave of snickers crosses real audience.

Close-up of hero from behind
as he stops, lights cigarette.

Silence.

Enduring shot of hero stumbling away, across snowfield,
finally disappearing into white distance.

Silence.   Profound silence.   Snow.   Dwarf pines.   Sky.

Shadow of mike boom appears on white snow.
Laughter.
Applause Noise, Applause Noise.

Shadow disappears.

Cut to hero spreading out sleeping bag in snow.
Wind machine starts up.
Hero puts out cigarette in snow. Loud sizzle.

Film breaks.

Screen audience boos, stomps feet:
real audience mutters approval.

Real film breaks.
Real audience boos—laughter mixed in.
Real film starts up again.

Fight scene starts in screen audience.

Applause Noise!
Mike boom itself appears in upper right of theatre,
just above fight.

Real audience whistles, laughs.
Mike boom disappears.

On screen, house lights dim, audience settles down, fight scene
    stops,
film starts up again.
Real audience boos.

Hero puts out cigarette in snow, loud sizzle,
inches into sleeping bag
goes to sleep teeth chattering.

Switch to hand-held camera.

Hand-held close-up of hero's big face twitching in cold sleep

Hero sleeps for a long time.   Sleeps.   Sleeps.

Tumbling feeling! Tumbling feeling!
Hero and sleeping bag tumbling across screen into snow!
Screen whites out!   Silence!

Audiences figure out cameraman has dropped camera into snow.
Laughter in real audience. Applause Noise!
Screen audience murmurs.

Two huge black-gloved fingers fill screen,
wipe snow from lens.

More laughter. Howls in real audience.
Screen audience grows entirely silent.

Much jiggling;
camera finally refocuses on sleeping hero.

Hero wakes up;
crawls reluctantly out of sleeping bag to pee,
does prat-fall on ice.

Uproar of laughter from real audience.
Screen audience begins to weep.

Asst. Film Editor credit flashes on screen, flashes off.

Screen audience bursts into uncontrollable fits of tears.
Hysterical laughter from real audience.

Entire teary-eyed screen audience turns in their seats
and glares at real audience.

Real audience quiets down quick—gets very nervous.

Hero disappears into snowy distance leaving sleeping bag
and torn coat behind.

Screen audience stares and stares at real audience.

Real audience begins to fade, begins to disappear.
Entire screen audience giggles, shouts in unison:

HA HA YOU ASSHOLES, SO LONG!

White out! Entire real audience whites-out!

Uproar of laughter from screen audience.
Theme comes up, wind dies, snow melts,
cut to hero who has made it back to civilization. Film ends.
House lights come up. Applause Noise. Applause Noise.

Screen audience puts on coats, lights cigarettes, ambles down aisles
out of theatre. Outside it has begun to snow.

Silence.

Real theme comes up, film ends, silence.
Curtain falls, silence.

The projectionist puts on his torn coat
alone in all the world
rethreads the projector
puts out cigarette in the snow. Loud sizzle.

Sticks head out of small square hole
high, high above empty theatre

shouts:

"Applause Noise! Applause Noise!"

A NOTE ABOUT THE AUTHOR

Anthony Sobin teaches in the Graduate Writing Program at Wichita State University, and is an editor of *The Ark River Review*. He has published both poetry and fiction in a variety of journals including *The American Poetry Review*, *Poetry Northwest*, *Paris Review*, *Partisan Review*, *Poetry*, and *New Letters*.